ANOTHER HARD DAY
AT THE ORIFICE

First published in Great Britain in 2004
by Ottakar's

Cover and design by Peter Wilkinson
Layout by seagulls
Printed in Thailand by Imago

INTRODUCTION

The photographs in this book cover a range of subjects
but they have two things in common. The first is that
they were all taken in the 'workplace', so to speak, be it a
vet's surgery or a school playground, a packing room or
a production line. And the second is that it was a happy
chance that the photographer was there at the right
time, at the right place to get the right photograph:
serendipity.

The image that appears in a photograph may be, by
accident, quite different from the one the photographer
had in mind when he pointed the camera and said, 'Say
cheese!' The perspective might bring the subjects closer
together or drive them further apart. A trick of the light
might change a sitter out of all recognition. That said, a

clever photographer can use perspective and light to create an image that is totally different from the one the subject had in mind when he or she agreed to be frozen for a moment in time by the camera.

In many cases, though, the subject matter is itself bizarre and arresting: a zoo keeper trying to push an elephant through a small opening; a London policeman issuing a traffic ticket to a knight in armour astride his charger; a man with a pressure washer giving Lord Nelson a clean high above Trafalgar Square.

Whatever the occupation, it helps to cast the world of work in a new and wholly unexpected light.

JUMBO SQUEEZE ON THE WAY

Whoever designed the entrance to the inside of the elephant house at London Zoo in the 1930s obviously didn't measure up to the job. If he (and in the far-off days of the 1930s it's more or less certain that it was a he) had got his sums right, the poor keeper would not have such a mammoth tusk in hand in getting his charge through the door to the sleeping quarters for a quick forty winks. And stuck in this position, one can only hope for the keeper's sake that the beast has no passing business on its mind.

JUMBO SQUEEZE
ON THE WAY

BALANCING THE SEATING ARRANGEMENTS

Seating arrangements, as every hostess knows,
can be a handful of trouble. But rarely are they a
mouthful! It takes years of training to learn to balance
one chair in the mouth. But 22, weighing a total of
almost 100 kilograms! That's how Latvian-born Fred
Loney earned his living when he worked for Tom
Arnold's Circus in the 1950s.

The days of travelling circuses are almost gone and
a sight like this a thing of the past. So let's raise a
glass to Loney and his likes. Cheers! Sorry: Chairs!

BALANCING
THE SEATING ARRANGEMENTS

NINE

'SOMETHING TO HOLD IT IN PLACE, SIR'

Male grooming is one of the boom industries of recent years. Men who a few years before would have regarded lotions and potions as far too girlie even to consider opening – never mind using – now cleanse, tone and moisturise with the best of them, and gel their hair into ever more exotic styles.

But there's nothing new under the sun. Eighty years ago there were many men who were willing to sit under curious contraptions like this one to have their hair permed to perfection.

Plus ça change, plus c'est la même poseur.

'SOMETHING TO HOLD
IT IN PLACE, SIR'

MONKEY BUSINESS BOOSTS TURNOVER

Being among our closest relatives in the natural world, chimpanzees suffer from many of the same health problems as we do – stress, indigestion, in-growing toenails, and don't even mention bad breath!

And while most monkeys have to grin and bare it when it comes to toothache, there are a few pampered primates who are sent by their indulgent owners for an annual check-up at the dentist.

One wonders if Sally, the chimp in the picture, will nod guiltily like so many of us when the dentist asks her the fateful 'Now, have we been flossing regularly?' question.

MONKEY BUSINESS BOOSTS TURNOVER

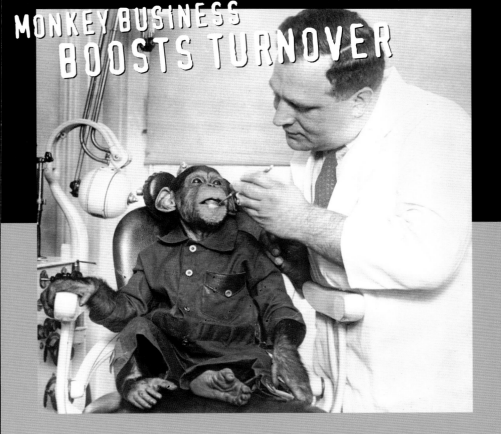

A MAN WITH A HEAD FOR BITES

Ever since Daniel bearded the lion in the den of biblical times, many men have attempted to emulate him, and many have died in the attempt. Let's hope that the brave (some would say foolhardy) lion tamer in this picture hasn't bitten off more than he can chew. Or indeed that the lion isn't tempted to chew off whatever he can bite.

Cynics may think that the lion's teeth have been drawn or dulled to make the stunt safe. Not so. His trainer is certain that despite a lot of growls and roars, the beast is quite tame. If he's wrong, of course, he's about to lose face in front of the audience!

A MAN WITH A
HEAD FOR BITES

FIFTEEN

THE LADY TAKES THE WRAP

She may be a dummy who spends all her time in shops, but this mannequin knows how to relax while others do the work. And in 1959, when public modesty was taken for granted, her two 'dressers' at this Surrey factory are scrupulous in ensuring that their charge is suitably attired before she ventures into the wider world.

In the good old days when there was only one class of post they could have been more or less certain that each model in their care would arrive at her destination the following day.

How times have changed.

THE LADY TAKES THE WRAP

YOU SCRATCH MY BACK …

It's fitting that it is in England – where the first dinosaur remains to be identified as such were discovered early in the nineteenth century by Gideon Mantell, a Sussex doctor – that huge, life-size models of these 'terrible lizards' are scattered around London's Crystal Palace Park.

And someone's got to clean them.

But one wonders if the man atop this huge armour-plated beast realised what he was taking on when he answered an ad in the Situations Vacant column of his local paper for a cleaning job. Perhaps the position was for a model cleaner: something he considered himself to be – in another sense of the word!

YOU SCRATCH MY BACK...

SMILE FOR THE CAMERA

History doesn't record what the young lady about to be X-rayed is suffering from, but judging from her perfect make-up, it doesn't look too life threatening.

Which is more than can be said for the machine in which she is lying. Shrouded in lead-lined curtains to protect the radiologist from the harmful effects of the rays, it looks for all the world like one of those contraptions illusionists use when they saw a lady in half.

Well, that would be another way of getting to the inside of the problem!

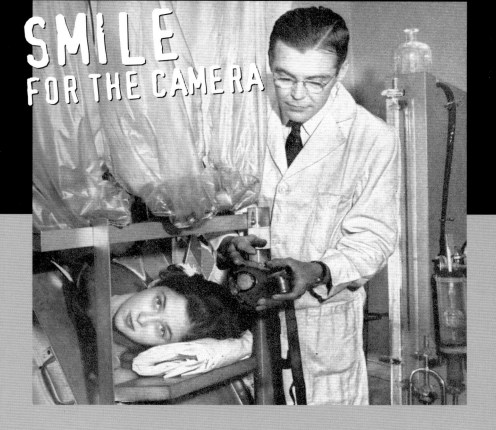

SMILE
FOR THE CAMERA

IMMERSED IN HIS JOB

It may look for all the world like someone is being dispatched to a watery grave. But it's not this world that these men have in mind, it's the next!

Members of the Jehovah's Witness movement believe that the end is nigh for everyone except the select few who will be chosen after Armageddon when Satan will be routed by the Risen Lord – any day now.

Baptism into the movement is by total immersion, as happened at this 1974 witness convention at Twickenham. A special tank was set up for the ceremony at London's hallowed rugby stadium where conversions of a Jonny Wilkinson kind are more frequently on display.

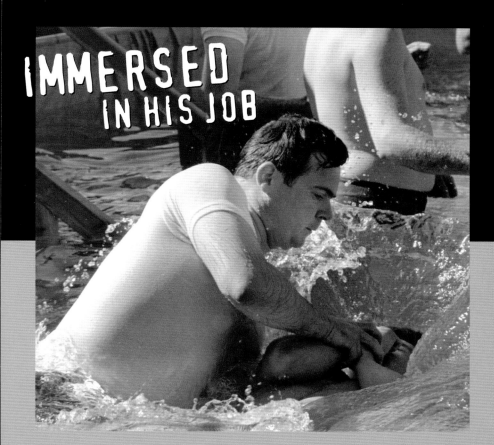

IMMERSED
IN HIS JOB

TWENTY THREE

GIRLS WITH THEIR HEADS IN BOOKS

Modelling in the 1920s was a far cry from the glamorous world of today's fashion milieu where top models sashay down the catwalk, a sultry pout on the lips and a couture confection on the hips.

Eighty years ago, many would-be Jody Kidds and Kate Mosses flocked to London to study at one of the several academies that taught modelling and deportment to *polite* young ladies.

How comforting for their mothers to know that among the many skills their daughters learned was how to balance the books, something their 'gals' would need to know when they came down to earth and married the nice, sensible chaps they met at the last tennis-club dance.

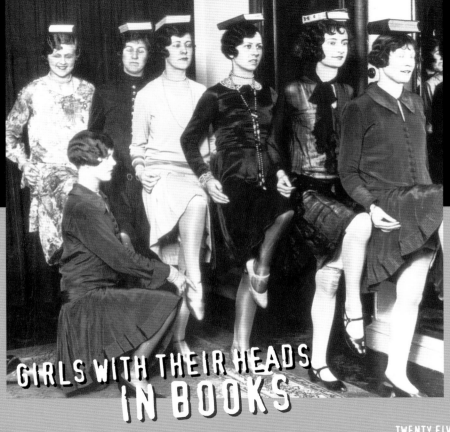

GIRLS WITH THEIR HEADS IN BOOKS

TWENTY FIVE

THE GAME'S A FOOT ...

A foot*ball* in the case of these Sisters of the Adoration of the Sacred Heart of Jesus of Montmartre.

Living at their Tyburn convent a stone's throw from London's Marble Arch, when the good sisters set aside their devotions for a few minutes every day, they like nothing better than bending it like Beckham or passing it like Pelé.

Rain stopping play is a cue for striking a different kind of ball – on the snooker table – but the sisters much prefer it when a spot of the beautiful game is the order of the day.

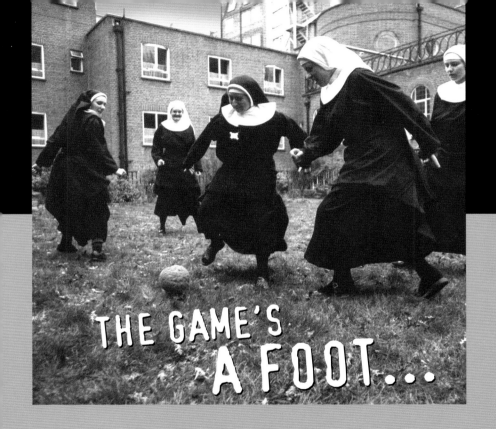

THE GAME'S A FOOT...

WALLPAPER OF NOTE

Ancient Egyptian kings paid craftsmen to decorate the walls of their pyramids. The Romans employed artists to create stunning mosaics, such as those at Ravenna in Italy that continue to captivate us today. The popes commissioned masters of their art such as Michelangelo to adorn their chapels. The Victorians lined their parlours with heavily embossed wallpapers. And German decorators of the 1920s …

In the years following World War I, the value of the Reichsmark plummeted. In one month alone in 1923, it fell from 10,000 to the US dollar to 50,000. So rather than lining their pockets with the worthless notes, many Germans used them to line their walls instead.

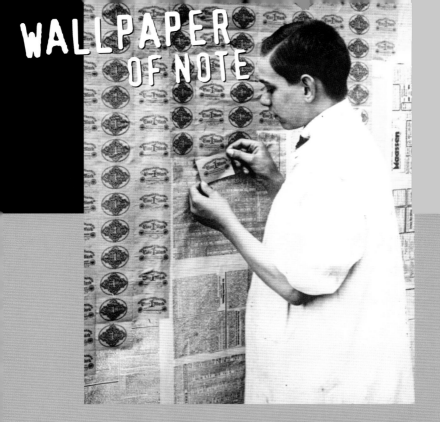

WALLPAPER
OF NOTE

SUSPICIONS OVER NEW SEASON TICKETS

The world of art offers a host of job opportunities. At the top of the pile there are the curatorships of the major collections. At a more humble level, it is the lot of auction house porters to move the goods on offer into place and carry them off to be delivered to the successful bidder.

During World War II, it was these porters who carried many of the treasures of London's art galleries to a huge vault below Piccadilly Circus tube station, safe from Hitler's bombs.

The war over, the paintings were returned whence they belonged. But didn't anyone tell the porters how annoying Londoners find it when escalators are blocked – even by work of art worth a king's ransom?

SUSPICIONS OVER NEW
SEASON TICKETS

GOING SWIMMINGLY

There can be very few of us who have not benefited from at least one member of the teaching profession, and today's teachers are a much more approachable bunch than the schoolmarms and masters of days gone by. It would never have entered the mind of the young man overseeing this swimming class to get down on his knees and join in. Chances are that a twenty-first century teacher would be in there, with his charges.

Mind you, chances are that a twenty-first century teacher would have a pool at his disposal, rather than having to resort to this waterless method of swimming instruction.

GOING SWIMMINGLY

THIRTY THREE

GETTING AHEAD WITH HIS JOB

The art of ventriloquism dates back to the sixth century BC when it was used by seers who claimed to be able to communicate with the dead. But the man in this photograph was concerned with 'seeing' of another kind. He was convinced that by marrying photography and telegraphy it would be possible to let people see what was happening as it was happening although they were nowhere near.

He's John Logie Baird, the man who invented television, seen here using ventriloquists' dummies in one of the many experiments that helped him to realise his dream, something he did in 1925.

He went on to show that it was possible to beam pictures across the Atlantic, and later to show that colour television was a practical proposition. Like all inventors, Baird was a man of vision: in his case, television.

GETTING AHEAD
WITH HIS JOB

ONE IN THE EAR FOR NELSON

Until recently the statue of Lord Nelson that dominates London's Trafalgar Square – as surely as the admiral's ships mastered the oceans during the Napoleonic Wars and the good admiral himself commanded Emma Hamilton's affections – was much marked by pigeon droppings.

The statue was, and still is, coated with an anti-pigeon gel to prevent London's flying vermin from doing too much damage to milord's noble features. Recently, thanks to restrictions on feeding the birds in the Square, there are far fewer pigeons than there used to be and consequently less damaging guano.

Even so, Richard Paffett and others like him regularly climb up the column to make sure that statues such as these are kept in shipshape condition.

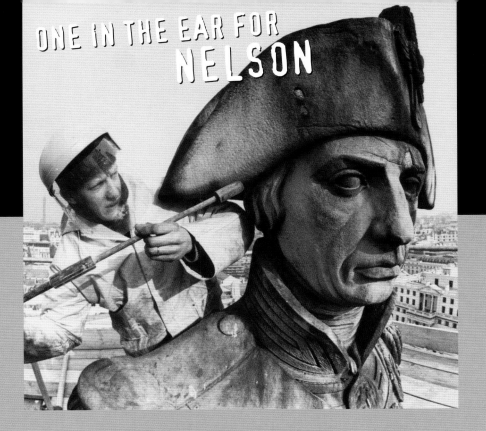

ONE IN THE EAR FOR NELSON

THIRTY SEVEN

'JUST A LITTLE JAB. PROMISE!'

The 'Roaring Twenties' were a great age of innovation. Hardly a day went by but a revolutionary new household device hit the headlines, a life-changing new invention announced. Some were a genuine boon. Others were as wacky as the races of a later day.

The dental lamp being demonstrated belonged to the first category. By allowing dentists to shine a light into the darker recesses of the mouth and nip potential trouble spots in the bud it helped to move dentistry out of the dark ages. Then a prospect of a visit to the dentist had the teeth chattering with fear. Today, there is little to be afraid of in a visit to a dentist. What with all the brushing and flossing, most of us have much better teeth than our grandparents, although it would be nice to think we shall all live to be as long in the tooth as they did.

'JUST A LITTLE JAB. PROMISE!'

'GOT IT!'

With the spread of light industry throughout Europe in the 1920s, but particularly in the United Kingdom, more and more workers found themselves poring over a hot lathe all day. These machines often caused tiny, sometimes microscopic, splinters of metal to lodge themselves in the operators' skin.

In 1927, some bright spark came up with the idea of using light rays to help detect these little shards. Once spotted, they could be painlessly removed with tweezers – at least that was the idea. The unfortunate victim seen here doesn't seem all that convinced.

Neither do the nurses come to that!

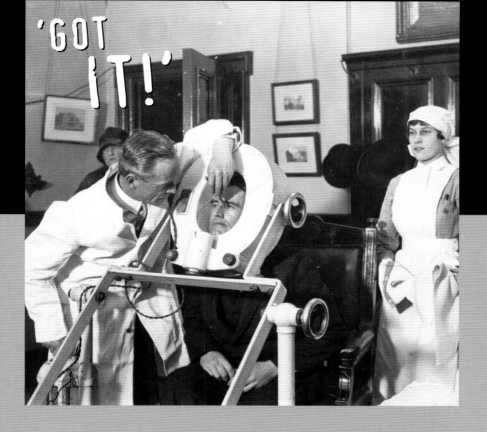

'GOT IT!'

WORKING ON THE CHAIN GANG

The expression 'chain gang' has its roots in the United States where convicted prisoners often found themselves linked together in irons as they got on with whatever mindless tasks their captors put them to.

The only crime the men in this picture committed was to find themselves in the pool of unskilled labour that existed in Wales in the decade after World War I. Life in the chain maker's yard in which they beat the heavy links into shape was the same day after day after mindless day.

One can't help but wonder if these men sympathised with Karl Marx who, in his *Manifesto* of the Communist Party, wrote, 'The workers have nothing to lose but their chains.'

WORKING ON THE
CHAIN GANG

FORTY THREE

GETTING OFF TO A FLYING START

The fact that whippet racing was often illegal because it attracted sometimes surprisingly heavy trackside betting did little to diminish the popularity of the sport in the north of England in the 1920s and 30s.

A good dog was worth good money, and competition among owners was intense. They threw themselves into the sport. And they often threw their dogs into it as well – quite literally as this picture shows. There was nothing in the rule book (if indeed there was one) to stop a handler holding a hound by the tail and ears and throwing it across the start line on the 'off', giving the dog a head start.

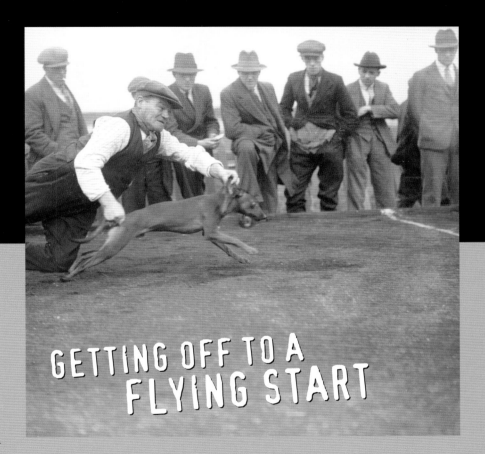

GETTING OFF TO A
FLYING START

TRUNK CALL

Elephants, they say, never forget. Let's hope this proud performer from a 1928 London circus remembers that its keeper had washed, fed and cared for it. And let's hope that the keeper *has* washed, fed and cared for the beast and it is not tempted to close its mighty mouth on the apparently foolhardy man who has put his life in his charge's jaws.

If not, then what looks like a trunk call (does anyone remember trunk calls?) might turn out to be a very close call indeed.

TRUNK CALL

A LOAD OF BOLOGNAISE

Spaghetti doesn't grow on trees, although thirty or so years ago, a memorable *Panorama* programme (broadcast by the BBC on 1 April) almost convinced half the population of the United Kingdom that it did.

Some pasta is made in the old way, by hand, in Italian kitchens, following recipes handed from generation to generation. But most of what we buy in our supermarkets is mass-produced.

Flour, water, salt, dried egg and whatever is fed into a vast hopper and mixed into a dough, which is itself fed through the machine to come out the other end as endless tubes of, in this case, macaroni.

In the days before the process was completely mechanised, someone had to make sure that each ribbon was separate from the others.

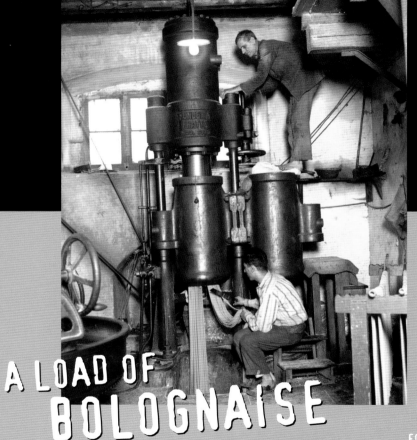

A LOAD OF
BOLOGNAISE

SOMETHING FOR THE WEAK END, SIR

It's not so long ago that barbers offered minor surgery as part of their service – the traditional red-and-white barber's pole is symbolic of just how bloody a simple short back and sides could be!

It could be quite an electrifying experience too, especially after one particular Sweeny Todd had the hair-raising idea of subjecting his customers to a small electric shock to make their hair stand on end, and, consequently, easier to cut.

Chemical hair-straightener has somehow never looked quite so appealing!

SOMETHING FOR THE
WEAK END,
SIR

A LITTLE DOWN IN THE MOUTH

A merchant seaman having a tooth extracted?
A stevedore being treated for bad breath? Neither!

The unfortunate man with his jaws agape is a
professional footballer. And the man putting a steel tube
in his mouth is administering a flu jab, 1920s' style.

In 1918, a worldwide flu epidemic killed many times
more people than were mindlessly slaughtered in four
years of fighting during World War I. Several years later
when another wave of the flu bug threatened to sweep
in from the East, prevention became the order of the
day. The team doctor tending to one of his charges is
determined that none of his men will fall victim to this
particular flu bug. By gum he is!

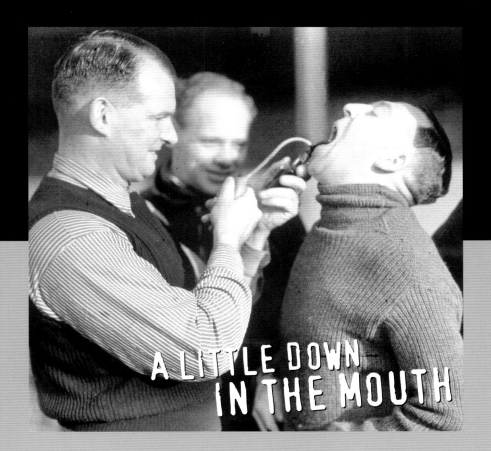

A LITTLE DOWN IN THE MOUTH

FIFTY THREE

EYES DOWN!

The girls with their heads in the butts and their butts in the air are lining the barrels with salt, ready to be filled with herring when the herring fleet sails back into Great Yarmouth.

The days when herring was a staple of the diet of working people are long gone. So, too, are the days when the old phrase 'there are plenty more fish in the sea' could be taken literally. Stocks of cod and other long-established favourites have been battered – by overfishing, rather than in the local chippie – and many a gourmet now extols the virtues of species previously unheard of by most of us. So perhaps the humble herring will have its day again, and we'll roll out the barrels once more.

EYES DOWN!

TAKE A WETTER, MISS GOOTCH

Inside countless city offices, in the days before computers replaced typewriters and air conditioning saw off fans, row after row of girls sweated over their typewriters transcribing their Pitman squiggles into perfectly typed correspondence, with a file copy faithfully recorded thanks to the use of carbon paper.

On a hot, sunny, sultry day what better way of keeping cool than heading outdoors and taking your work with you? That's what these two girls have done. Off with the dresses, on with the swimsuits and once they had typed the last 'I remain, Sir, Your obedient servant' they no doubt dived from their makeshift typing pool into the cool waters of the adjacent swimming pool.

TAKE A WETTER,
MISS GOOTCH

TOO MANY CHEFS . . .

All that tasting and sampling from breakfast through to dinner! No wonder so many chefs pile on the pounds and could do with going on a diet and exercise regime.

No one recalls whose brainwave it was, but around 1930, someone had the idea to summon chefs from restaurants around Piccadilly Circus and put them through their paces on the roof of the Trocadero Building early one morning.

Bending this way and that can be exhausting work, and certainly does make a man think about his joints – of beef, and mutton and pork probably!

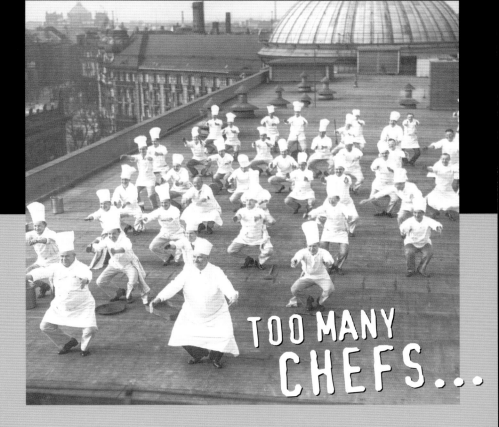

TOO MANY
CHEFS...

UPSTAIRS ONLY!

London's 31 bus winds its way from leafy Chelsea to recently gentrified Camden Town, a route that takes it past Earl's Court, one of the capital's major exhibition and pop-concert venues.

Over the years, the conductors who work the route have had to cope with screaming Spice Girls fans, Rolling Stones freaks, the usual assortment of London characters, rich tourists weighed down with shopping bags emblazoned with the names of the capital's smarter shops and young ones with little money and large rucksacks – and a succession of circuses.

It would be nice to think that this is Nellie, the trunk-packing heroine of the song long-popular with children. It's not, of course. It was the idea of the publicity people at David Smart's Circus.

Hope someone warned the conductor!

UPSTAIRS ONLY!

GOING ROUND IN CIRCLES!

Many and varied have been the devices dreamt up by man to get him around. From Leonardo's visionary designs for a helicopter, which would have taken off, to Clive Sinclair's one-man car, which sadly didn't – at least not in a commercially successful way – there must have been literally thousands of bright ideas. Many of them never got off the drawing board. This one did, though.

The Dynasphere, an electrically powered wheel that could be driven at up to 30 mph, was the invention of a certain J. A. Purves and his son, of Taunton, in Devon. Seen here putting his creation through its paces on the beach at Weston-super-Mare, Purves seems determined to prove that some inventions are destined to do the rounds.

GOING ROUND IN CIRCLES!

IN SOMETHING OF A TEAT SPOT

This impromptu event happened in 1960 outside London's Royal Exchange where the fifth Dairy Festival was being held. Woburn Bibby was in town from Bedford for a short stay.

We can only hazard a guess at what is on the policeman's mind as he watches a herdsman milking a Jersey cow on the streets of London. Thinking of giving him a parking ticket perhaps? A warning that 'You can't do that sort of thing here, Sir.' Or a warning that the authorities take a very dim view of anyone who makes a living out of milking London's tourists.

IN SOMETHING OF A
TEAT SPOT

MEN WITH TIME ON THEIR HANDS

Officially it's the Clock Tower, or St Stephen's, at the Palace of Westminster. Countless millions of people around the world know it better as Big Ben, after the huge bell it houses. And like any building situated in the city centre with traffic roaring past it 24 hours a day, it needs a good clean every now and then to keep it in pristine condition.

With no ladder long enough to reach the clock face from street level, there is only one way for the cleaners to get to the thick glass face and give it a good scrub. From the top down.

In the words of one passer-by who looked up and saw the men at work – 'rather them than me'.

MEN WITH TIME ON THEIR HANDS

MIX IT, SISTER

When money's tight and there's not enough in the convent kitty to pay for the leak in the chapel roof let alone a new swimming pool, what's a nun to do?

There's prayer, of course. And the Good Lord always answers our prayers. But he's just as likely to say, 'No!' as 'Yes!'.

So when the sisters of the Franciscan Missionaries of the Divine Motherhood thought that they would like a swimming pool at their Surrey convent during the sizzling summer of 1976, and funds were short, there was nothing for it. They rolled up their sleeves, hired a cement mixer and got digging and mixing.

Cool!

MIX IT, SISTER

SKELETON CREW

We know that traffic in London, as in so many cities round the world, has become so bad that many journeys seem to take forever, but this is ridiculous!

As usual, all is not what it seems, though.

The skeleton pictured here is not some relic from the crypt, it's a plastic replica being taken from the factory in Croydon in south London to one of the city's hospitals where it will be used to teach medical students basic anatomy.

But how many of us when stuck in a traffic jam on our ever-busier roads, have been forced, like this skeleton, to sit there, grin and bare it.

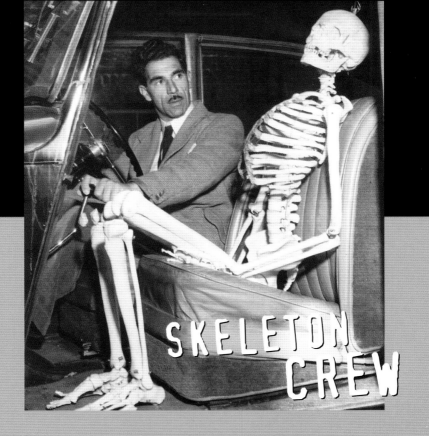

SKELETON CREW

>WEATHERVANE GILDER

NICE ONE, WILLIAM!

Has some latter-day William Tell misfired his arrow and landed it way off target? It may be nice to think so, but the truth is much more mundane.

When the weather vane atop the clock tower at London's King's Cross Station became so covered in grime that it was rendered almost invisible against the cloud-heavy sky, someone had to climb up and re-gild it, so that Londoners could see which way the wind was blowing.

Some men get to the top of their profession by climbing the ladder. This man has to climb to the top of the ladder simply to get on top of his job.

NICE ONE,
WILLIAM!

'MOBILE PHONES? NO FUTURE.'

Invented in 1876 by Alexander Graham Bell, the telephone revolutionised personal communications. By the 1920s most people in the western word, if they didn't have a telephone, had access to one via the call boxes that were installed on the streets of the towns and villages where they lived.

Telephone design has come a long way since then. Gone are the separate earpiece and voice box of this jumbo-size model being taken to an Ideal Home Exhibition in 1928. Today's phones fit snugly into the palms of our hands. And when we press button A it's not to get connected, it's as part of a text message.

Goodbye 'Testing! Testing!' Hello 'Texting! Texting!'

'MOBILE PHONES?
NO FUTURE.'

'AND THE MILKMAID PLAYETH BLITHE . . .'

Three hundred years after John Milton had his *L'Allegro* milkmaid 'singing blithe', Surrey farmer's wife Nora Johnston decided to add a little *allegro* of her own to the daily milking.

Convinced that contented cows gave higher milk yields, she hauled her portable carillon – a set of bells played from a keyboard and/or pedals – into the field and struck up the band.

The records do not record her repertoire, but when Mrs Johnston was around, it's probably safe to say that the hills were alive with the sound of music.

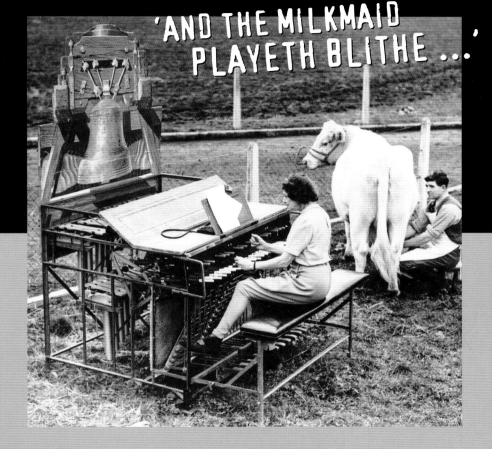

'AND THE MILKMAID PLAYETH BLITHE ...'

SEVENTY SEVEN

A HIGHLY STRUNG WOMAN

Sadly, the days when thousands of East Enders decamped to the Garden of England to spend the season working in the hop fields are long gone. Today, specialist machines and foreign students have replaced the cockney families, but there are still many older people who were born within the sound of the Bow Bells who remember the good old days.

The woman in this picture sports the strings to be used for attaching hop bines to the wires and does so with all the style and aplomb of a Parisian fashion model. A genuine Bow Belle.

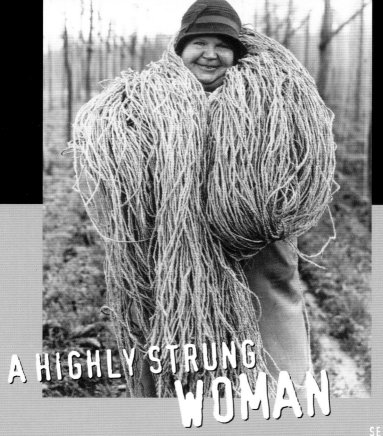

A HIGHLY STRUNG WOMAN

BASKET CASES

Looking for all the world as if they have stepped straight from the pages of *Gulliver's Travels* when he was in Lilliput, it's not the men who are small, it's the baskets that are huge.

They (the baskets) were not destined to be used by heavy shoppers. Once work on them had finished, they were shipped to South Africa where they were used for loading oil cake – stock feed consisting of compressed cubes made from the residue of the crushed seeds of oil-bearing crops such as linseed.

BASKET
CASES

ARE BUS FARES A FLEECE?

Mary may have had a little lamb, and it may have
followed her to school one day. But that's nothing on
Marjorie Dare, a 1930s' miss who also had a little lamb.
We don't know if it followed her to school, but we do
know that it followed her most everywhere else.

What the bus conductor thought of it is not on record.
Did he try to ram it into the space under the stairs set
aside for luggage and heavy bags? And as for the other
passengers, one can't help wondering if they looked
a little sheepish when they saw what was following
Miss Dare onto the bus.

ARE BUS FARES A FLEECE?

A HECK OF A MOUTHFUL

London's world-famous Zoo is more than a place to which people flock to see one of the best and best-kept collections of animals anywhere in the world. It is a centre of scientific excellence and research that has added a vast amount to our store of knowledge about the animal kingdom.

Its keepers are dedicated to the animals in their charge and know them probably as well as they know their own families. When a bird or beast is off colour, chances are its keeper will be the first to notice. It looks like that's what's happened here: something's been tickling the big-beaked bird's throat, and the keeper is the first to try to get to the root of the problem.

Either that, or the keeper put his lunch down somewhere and he's looked everywhere else …

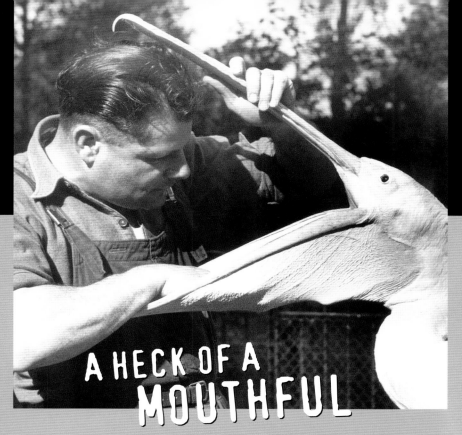

A HECK OF A
MOUTHFUL

WHEN A MAN'S GOT TO GO . . .

The official line is that the men in this picture are
testing tyres in the early months of World War II when
some boffin or other had come up with a new, and
top-secret method of making them bullet-proof.
One can only wonder what kind of military vehicles
they were designed for

But how are they being tested? Aye, there's the rub (-ber).

It looks for all the world as if the men in charge of them
had a more pressing need than testing tyres and had
rushed to the first private spot to alleviate the pressure.

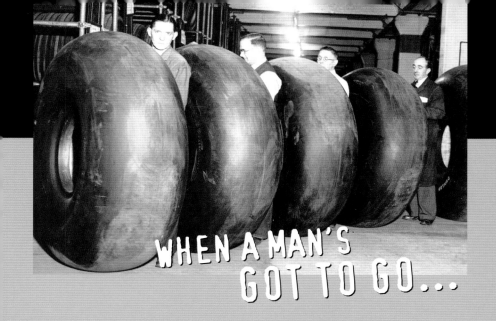

WHEN A MAN'S
GOT TO GO...

UP FOR GRABS

Demolition contractors have been hard at work for thousands of years. In Old Testament times, according to the book of Judges, Samson did a very thorough job on the Philistines' temple.

Since then, whenever technology has made it possible for taller and bigger buildings to be erected, it's out with the old as gangs of demolition workers move in to prepare the ground for the new.

The job is not without risks, of course, but there's little danger of this unsuspecting worker falling prey to the alien-like claw that seems to be about to take him into its lethal grip.

The two are probably some distance apart – as long as we get things in perspective.

UP FOR GRABS

EIGHTY NINE

THE LEAGUE OF CANE-INE DEFENCE

In the bad old days (?) before corporal punishment was abolished in all local authority and most public schools in the UK, there was a steady demand in England for canes for the administration thereof to the bottoms and hands of miscreant schoolboys. (Things were different in Scotland where a two-tongued leather strap known as 'the tawse' was used to ensure classroom discipline.)

Before a cane worthy of respect was put on sale it was tested for strength, length and pliability, as seen in this photograph taken at the height of the 'swinging sixties' at a factory in Sussex, which produced 15,000 canes each year.

Here was another industry that disappeared with education reforms.

THE LEAGUE OF
CANE-INE DEFENCE

A KNIGHT TO REMEMBER

1956 may seem a far cry from the early years of the 21st century but even half a century ago knights in armour astride their chargers were not a common sight on the streets of London. However, all men are equal before the law and when this splendidly apparelled evocation of the Middle Ages appeared on the streets of Kensington he was promptly booked by a diligent London bobby for committing a traffic offence.

This booking must also have seemed a trifle unwelcoming to Mr Kenneth Quicke, the 'knight' in shining armour, who had just ridden 140 miles from Staffordshire on a goodwill trip that culminated in a visit to the opening of the Electrical Engineers Exhibition.

A KNIGHT TO REMEMBER

LUNCHING WITH THE HIGH-FLIERS

Over the years waiters in New York City have become used to catering to bizarre requests from their clientele, but even the most urbane Manhattan maitre d' could be forgiven for showing some surprise when asked to send a couple of his staff to serve lunch on a building site – especially when that site was several hundred feet above the teeming streets of Midtown.

Undeterred, however, the two doughty waiters pictured here ascended the skeleton of the city's latest skyscraper in November 1930 to serve lunch to a couple of steel workers seated astride a girder high above the Big Apple. We can only hope that the meal they presented lived up to the diners' high expectations.

LUNCHING WITH THE
HIGH-FLIERS

PICTURE CREDITS

The publishers would like to thank the following agencies
for permission to reproduce their images:

Royal Veterinary College/Wellcome Photo Library: Cover

Hulton Archive/Getty Images: Pages seven, nine, eleven, thirteen,
seventeen, nineteen, twenty three, twenty five, twenty nine, thirty three,
thirty five, thirty nine, forty one, forty three, forty five, forty seven, forty nine,
fifty one, fifty three, fifty five, fifty seven, fifty nine, sixty one, sixty three,
sixty five, sixty seven, sixty nine, seventy one, seventy three, seventy five,
seventy seven, seventy nine, eighty one, eighty three, eighty five,
eighty seven, ninety one, ninety three, ninety five

The Times: Pages twenty seven and thirty seven

The Culture Archive: Page twenty one

SOA: Pages fifteen and eighty nine

TopFoto: Page thirty one